The route to your roots

When they look back at their formative years, many Indians nostalgically recall the vital part Amar Chitra Katha picture books have played in their lives. It was **ACK – Amar Chitra Katha** – that first gave them a glimpse of their glorious heritage.

Since they were introduced in 1967, there are now **over 400 Amar Chitra Katha** titles to choose from. **Over 90 million copies** have been sold worldwide.

Now the Amar Chitra Katha titles are even more widely available in **1000+ bookstores all across India**. Log on to www.ack-media.com to locate a bookstore near you. If you do not have access to a bookstore, you can buy all the titles through our online store **www.amarchitrakatha.com**. We provide quick delivery anywhere in the world.

To make it easy for you to locate the titles of your choice from our treasure trove of titles, the books are now arranged in five categories.

Epics and Mythology
Best known stories from the Epics and the Puranas

Indian Classics
Enchanting tales from Indian literature

Fables and Humour
Evergreen folktales, legends and tales of wisdom and humour

Bravehearts
Stirring tales of brave men and women of India

Visionaries
Inspiring tales of thinkers, social reformers and nation builders

Contemporary Classics
The Best of Modern Indian literature

Amar Chitra Katha Pvt Ltd

© Amar Chitra Katha Pvt Ltd, 2000, Reprinted December 2012, ISBN 978-81-8482-103-1
Published & Printed by Amar Chitra Katha Pvt. Ltd., Krishna House, 3rd Floor,
Raghuvanshi Mill Compound, S.B.Marg, Lower Parel (W), Mumbai- 400 013. India
For Consumer Complaints Contact Tel : +91-22 40497436
Email: customerservice@ack-media.com

The route to your roots

KRISHNA AND THE FALSE VAASUDEVA

Envy and flattery flourished at the court of the powerful King Vaasudeva. It was a dangerous combination. Vaasudeva became proud and boastful – only because he shared a name with the divine Krishna, also known as Vaasudeva. The foolish king considered himself the lord of the universe! Confusion and calamity resulted, and together made for a tale in the Bhagawat Purana, that is packed with humour and sound advice.

Script
Kamala Chandrakant

Illustrations
V.B.Halbe

Editor
Anant Pai

Cover illustration by: C.M.Vitankar

KRISHNA AND THE FALSE VAASUDEVA

A MESSENGER FROM JARASANDHA, THE EMPEROR OF MAGADHA, CAME TO THE COURT OF VAASUDEVA, THE MIGHTY, BUT STUPID KING OF PUNDRA *.

THE EMPEROR'S FAVOURITE VASSAL, LORD SHISHUPALA ⚕, IS GOING TO WED RUKMINI, THE PRINCESS OF VIDARBHA...

THAT PEERLESS BEAUTY! GOOD NEWS, INDEED!

THE EMPEROR WANTS ALL HIS ALLIES TO COME PREPARED FOR BATTLE. HE EXPECTS TROUBLE FROM THAT YADAVA, KRISHNA.◉

* MODERN NORTH BENGAL. ⚕ KING OF CHEDI ◉ ALSO KNOWN AS VAASUDEVA

BUT HASN'T RUKMI*PROMISED HIS SISTER TO SHISHUPALA?

HE HAS! AND THERE IS NOT GOING TO BE A SWAYAMVARA BUT...

...ONE CAN NEVER BE SURE! THE YADAVA MAY DECIDE THAT HE WANTS RUKMINI FOR HIMSELF.

NOT AS LONG AS I LIVE!

WHEN VAASUDEVA AND HIS ARMY REACHED VIDARBHA, JARASANDHA AND HIS ALLIES WERE ALREADY THERE. AMONG THEM WAS VAASUDEVA'S CLOSE FRIEND, THE KING OF KASHI.

EVERYTHING SEEMS TO BE ALL RIGHT. THERE IS NO SIGN OF THE YADAVA.

*RUKMINI'S BROTHER

EVEN IF HE DOES COME, WE WILL NOT LET HIM GET ANYWHERE NEAR THE PRINCESS. WE WILL NOT FAIL SHISHUPALA AND THE EMPEROR!

THE NEXT MORNING, SHISHUPALA AND THE ASSEMBLED KINGS WAITED PATIENTLY FOR RUKMINI TO EMERGE FROM THE TEMPLE WHERE SHE HAD GONE TO WORSHIP BEFORE THE WEDDING CEREMONY.

AS RUKMINI CAME OUT, SO DAZZLED WERE THEY BY HER BEAUTY THAT THEY STOOD STARING AT HER, HARDLY AWARE OF ANYTHING ELSE!

SUDDENLY, AS IF FROM NOWHERE, KRISHNA APPEARED IN HIS CHARIOT...

...WHISKED RUKMINI INTO IT...

...AND DROVE OFF!

STOP HIM!

HE HAS ABDUCTED THE PRINCESS!

LITTLE DID THEY REALISE THAT RUKMINI HAD MADE HER OWN CHOICE AND HER OWN PLANS.

AS THE STUPEFIED EMPEROR AND HIS ALLIES TRIED TO GIVE CHASE...

...THEY WERE CHECKED BY BALARAMA, KRISHNA'S MIGHTY BROTHER.

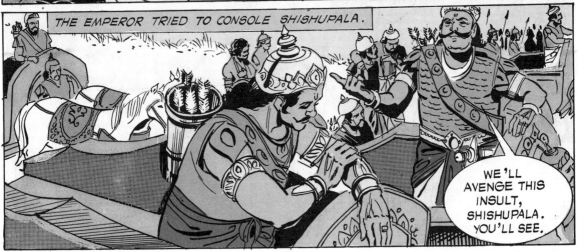

THE EMPEROR TRIED TO CONSOLE SHISHUPALA.

WE'LL AVENGE THIS INSULT, SHISHUPALA. YOU'LL SEE.

WHILE THE EMPEROR PLANNED REVENGE, VAASUDEVA RETURNED TO HIS CAPITAL, A DEJECTED MAN.

HE WAS ONE AND WE WERE MANY. YET HE CARRIED OFF RUKMINI! UNDER OUR VERY NOSE!

HIS COURTIERS WERE WORRIED.

THIS WILL NEVER DO! IF THE KING REMAINS SO LISTLESS, THE KINGDOM WILL BE OPEN TO IN-VADERS AND OUR PEOPLE WILL BECOME SLAVES.

IT'S THAT KRISHNA WHO HAS DONE THIS TO HIM.

YOU MEAN VAASUDEVA, THE SON OF THAT NOBLEMAN OF MATHURA?

YES! THE PEOPLE REVERE HIM AS LORD VISHNU HIMSELF COME DOWN TO EARTH. I'M SURE THAT IS WHAT MAKES HIM SO VAIN AND SELF-CONFIDENT.

SUDDENLY ONE OF THE COURTIERS SNAPPED HIS FINGERS.

I HAVE AN IDEA! WHY NOT PROCLAIM OUR KING THE LORD INCARNATE, AND KRISHNA AN IMPOSTOR?

IMPOSSIBLE! OUR KING HIMSELF WILL NOT BELIEVE IT.

WE ONLY HAVE TO CONVINCE THE PEOPLE AND SOON OUR KING WILL COME TO BELIEVE IT HIMSELF.

AND IN NO TIME HE WILL REGAIN HIS SELF-CONFIDENCE.

THE COURTIERS SET TO WORK.

...HE IS THE TRUE VAASUDEVA! KRISHNA IS AN IMPOSTOR!

IT CAN'T BE TRUE!

OUR KING IS VAASUDEVA, LORD VISHNU INCARNATE!

KRISHNA IS AN IMPOSTOR!

AS TIME ROLLED BY —

AM I REALLY LORD VISHNU INCARNATE? THE PEOPLE COULD NOT BE MISTAKEN. I MUST BE VISHNU REBORN.

AND THE KING BELIEVED HIMSELF TO BE VISHNU. AND HE BEGAN TO DRESS LIKE KRISHNA, THE VAASUDEVA.

HOW DARE THAT YADAVA CALL HIMSELF VAASUDEVA! THE IMPOSTOR!

AND THAT IMPOSTOR HAS MY DISCUS AND INSIGNIA.

10

ONE DAY—

GO TO DWARAKA AND GIVE KRISHNA THIS MESSAGE...

A FEW DAYS LATER AT DWARAKA—

LORD, AN AMBASSADOR FROM THE COURT OF VAASUDEVA, KING OF PUNDRA, SEEKS AN AUDIENCE.

SHOW HIM IN.

MY NAMESAKE IS AN ALLY OF JARASANDHA AND SHISHUPALA. WHAT COULD HE WANT WITH ME?

HIS QUESTION WAS SOON ANSWERED.

OUR DIVINE KING, VISHNU INCARNATE, SAYS: "COME TO PUNDRA AND GIVE UP MY DISCUS, YOU FOOLISH MAN. LAY ASIDE MY INSIGNIA AND MY NAME. IF YOU COME AND PAY HOMAGE TO ME, I WILL VOUCHSAFE YOUR SAFETY."

KRISHNA WAS AMUSED.

OH! SO THAT'S IT! VAASUDEVA HAS DIVINE DESIGNS!

GO TO VAASUDEVA AND TELL HIM THIS FROM ME...

WHEN THE MESSENGER RETURNED TO PUNDRA —

WHAT DID HE SAY? WAS HE ANGRY?

NO, MY LORD. HE SAID SINCE YOU COMMAND HIM TO COME, HE WILL OBEY IMMEDIATELY. HE WILL BRING THE DISCUS, HIS EMBLEM, AND CONSIGN IT TO YOU. AND···

··· SEEKING ASYLUM WITH YOU, HE WILL ENSURE THAT HE WILL NEVER MORE HAVE ANYTHING TO DREAD FROM YOU.

WHAT! IS KRISHNA GIVING IN SO EASILY? I AM INDEED FORTUNATE!

BUT HIS COURTIERS DID NOT THINK SO.

I DON'T TRUST THAT YADAVA!

YES. THERE IS MORE TO THIS THAN MEETS THE EYE!

WHY NOT SEND A MESSENGER TO THE KING OF KASHI AND SEEK HIS ADVICE? EVEN INDRA, KING OF THE DEVAS, FEARS HIM.

WHEN THE KING OF KASHI HEARD THE WHOLE STORY—

VAASUDEVA OF PUNDRA DOESN'T REALISE WHAT HE HAS DONE! WOULD HE WHO HAS HUMBLED THE EMPEROR HIMSELF SURRENDER TO A MERE KING AND SEEK HIS PROTECTION?

I HAD BETTER GO WITH MY TROOPS AND MYSELF TAKE ON THE REARGUARD. THE KING OF PUNDRA IS GOING TO NEED US.

HE SENT FOR HIS SON, SUDAKSHINA.

KRISHNA THE YADAVA, MUST BE TAUGHT A LESSON AND I AM GOING TO HELP THE KING OF PUNDRA TEACH IT TO HIM. LOOK AFTER THE KINGDOM WHILE I AM AWAY.

MEANWHILE KRISHNA, MOUNTED ON GARUDA, WAS WELL ON HIS WAY TO PUNDRA, WITH HIS MACE, DISCUS AND BOW.

AS HE NEARED THE CITY —

VAASUDEVA OF PUNDRA HAS UNDERSTOOD WHAT I MEANT.

AS THEY DREW NEARER, KRISHNA SAW VAASUDEVA, DRESSED EXACTLY LIKE HIMSELF.

HA! HA! HA! HO! HO!

LAUGHING ALL THE WHILE, KRISHNA ATTACKED.

SOON THE EARTH WAS STREWN WITH THE BODIES OF THE TWO ARMIES AND THEIR HORSES AND ELEPHANTS.

VAASUDEVA, YOU WANTED ME TO HAND OVER MY INSIGNIA!

BUT THE WARNING WAS TOO LATE. KRISHNA'S MACE HIT VAASUDEVA, HURLING HIM TO THE GROUND.

THE NEXT MOMENT THE DISCUS CUT HIS THROAT, AND VAASUDEVA WAS NO MORE.

THE GARUDA ON HIS BANNER WAS SHATTERED TO BITS BY KRISHNA'S GARUDA.

AS KRISHNA TURNED ROUND, THE KING OF KASHI ACCOSTED HIM.

WELL DONE, KRISHNA! BUT DON'T FORGET, I'M STILL ALIVE.

WHY DON'T YOU FIGHT ME, YOU IMPOSTOR?

KRISHNA ONLY SMILED IN REPLY...

...AND RAISING HIS BOW LET FLY AN ARROW.

THE NEXT MOMENT THE HEAD OF THE KING OF KASHI WAS SEVERED FROM THE BODY.

BUT THE MOMENTUM OF THE ARROW WAS SO GREAT THAT IT CARRIED THE HEAD OF THE KING WITH IT···

··· AND DISAPPEARED INTO SPACE.

A VICTORIOUS KRISHNA RETURNED TO DWARAKA WHERE HE WAS RECEIVED BY HIS REJOICING SUBJECTS.

MEANWHILE, THE ARROW CARRYING THE HEAD OF THE KING OF KASHI, WHIZZED THROUGH THE AIR...

...TILL IT REACHED THE PALACE GATES OF THE CITY OF KASHI.

OUR KING HAS BEEN SLAIN, ALAS!

ALAS!

ALAS!

WHEN SUDAKSHINA, THE SON OF THE KING OF KASHI, HEARD THEIR CRIES, HE CAME OUT OF THE PALACE.

IT IS THE WORK OF KRISHNA OF DWARAKA. I WILL NOT REST TILL I SEE HIM DEAD.

ALONG WITH HIS FAMILY PRIEST, SUDAKSHINA BEGAN TO PERFORM A YAGNA.

SWAHA!

SUDDENLY THE SACRIFICIAL FIRE BLAZED HIGH...

... AND FROM IT EMERGED A FORMIDABLE FEMALE, WITH FLAMES OF FIRE LEAPING OUT OF HER HAIR.

ROARING ANGRILY, SHE CHARGED THROUGH THE AIR TOWARDS DWARAKA.

MEANWHILE AT DWARAKA, KRISHNA WAS PLAYING DICE WITH RUKMINI.

SUDDENLY —

LORD SAVE US!

A FIERY FIEND IS HEADING TOWARDS DWARAKA.

SHE ROARS THAT SHE WON'T REST TILL DWARAKA WITH ALL ITS INHABITANTS IS RAZED TO THE GROUND.

TURNING, THE FIEND FLED.

BUT THE DISCUS PURSUED HER RELENTLESSLY.

AH! THE CITY OF SUDAKSHINA. SINCE IT WAS SUDAKSHINA WHO BROUGHT ME TO THIS PLIGHT, I WILL SLAY HIM.

MEANWHILE SUDAKSHINA AND HIS ARMIES HAD ALREADY BEGUN RESISTING THE DISCUS...

···BUT IN VAIN. THE DISCUS ATTACKED THEM WITH A VENGEANCE, FELLING THEM IN ALL DIRECTIONS. TILL···

···THE LAST OF SUDAKSHINA'S SOLDIERS FELL.

SUDAKSHINA FLED FROM THE BATTLE-FIELD TO HIS PALACE.

MEANWHILE THE FIEND TOO HAD REACHED THE PALACE.

YOU SHALL DIE FOR BEING THE CAUSE OF MY HUMILIATION!

AND SUDAKSHINA WAS BURNT TO DEATH BY THE CREATURE HIS OWN INCANTATIONS HAD BROUGHT FORTH.

SUDDENLY—

NO! IT'S THE SUDARSHANA-CHAKRA AGAIN! IT HAS PURSUED ME INTO THE CITY.

AS THE DISCUS APPROACHED, THE FIEND FLED...

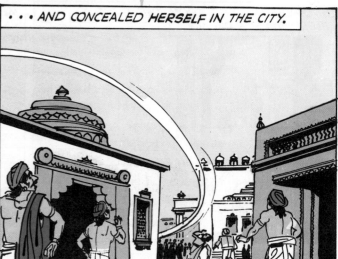

... AND CONCEALED HERSELF IN THE CITY.

THE BLAZING DISCUS WHIRRED THROUGH PALACE ASSEMBLY HALLS...

...THE ROYAL STABLES...

...THE COW-SHEDS...

...THE HOUSES...

...THE GRANARIES...

...AND THE MARKETS...

...TILL THE WHOLE CITY OF KASHI WAS WRAPPED UP IN FLAMES...

...WHICH CONSUMED EVEN THE FUGITIVE FIEND.

THE DISCUS, THEN, WITH UNMITIGATED VIGOUR AND BLAZING FIERCELY, WHIRLED AROUND AND...

...WHIZZED BACK TO THE PALACE AT DWARAKA...

...TO THE HANDS OF THE TRUE VAASUDEVA.

SUBSCRIBE NOW!

Pay only ₹~~1080~~ 800!

25% OFF

A twelve month subscription to **TINKLE** and **TINKLE DIGEST**

YOUR DETAILS*

Student's Name _____

Parent's Name _____

Date of Birth: _____ (DD MM YYYY)

Address: _____

_____

_____

City: _____ PIN: _____

State: _____

School: _____

Class: _____

Email (Student): _____

Email (Parent): _____

Tel of Parent: (R): _____

Mobile: _____

_____
Parent's Signature:
*All the above fields are mandatory for the subscription to get activated.

PAYMENT OPTIONS

☐ **Credit Card**
Card Type: Visa ☐ MasterCard ☐
Please charge ₹800 to my Credit Card Number
below:☐☐☐☐ ☐☐☐☐ ☐☐☐☐ ☐☐☐☐
Expiry Date: ☐☐ ☐☐

Cardmember's Signature:

☐ **CHEQUE / DD**
Enclosed please find cheque / DD no. ☐☐☐☐☐☐ drawn in
favour of "ACK Media Direct Pvt. Ltd."
on (bank) _____
for the amount _____, dated ☐☐/☐☐/☐☐☐☐ and
send it to: **IBH magazine Service, Arch no.30, Below
Mahalaxmi Bridge, Near Racecourse, Mahalaxmi,
Mumbai 400034**

☐ **Pay by VPP**
Please pay the ₹800 to the postman on the delivery
of 1st issue. (Additional charges ₹30 apply)

☐ **Online subscription**
Visit www.amarchitrakatha.com

For any queries or further information please
write to us ACK Media Direct Pvt. Ltd.,
Krishna House, 3rd Floor, Raghuvanshi Mills Compund,
Senapati Bapat Marg, Lower Parel, Mumbai 400 013.
Tel: 022-40 49 74 36
or send us an Email at customercare@ack-media.com

SUDAMA

THE POWER OF TRUE FRIENDSHIP

www.amarchitrakatha.com

The route to your roots

SUDAMA

Sudama's gift was small and inexpensive, but Krishna found it priceless as it came with selfless love. Krishna, who had both wealth and fame at his command, received it with pure joy. Life had taken the two friends on different paths, and Sudama was now painfully poor. Their affection overcame all differences, however. A simple meal became equal to a luxurious feast – and magically turned a poor hut into a mansion of gold.

Script
Kamala Chandrakant

Illustrations
Prabhakar Khanolkar

Editor
Anant Pai

SUDAMA AND KRISHNA HAD MET IN GURU SANDIPANI'S ASHRAM.

*A PLACE WHERE THE SACRED FIRE IS KEPT BURNING.

SUDAMA OFTEN PRACTISED WITH KRISHNA.

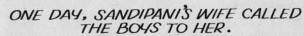
ONE DAY, SANDIPANI'S WIFE CALLED THE BOYS TO HER.

SOON AFTER THEY ENTERED THE FOREST...

...A TERRIBLE STORM BROKE OUT.

KRISHNA!

AT LAST THE STORM CLEARED, BUT NIGHT HAD FALLEN.

WE HAVE LOST OUR WAY.

DO NOT BE FRIGHTENED, SUDAMA. I AM WITH YOU.

I AM WORRIED ABOUT THE BOYS. I WILL GO AND LOOK FOR THEM.

LIFE IS DEAR TO ALL AND YET YOU HAVE DISREGARDED THAT LIFE FOR MY SAKE...

AND HE GRANTED THEM A BOON.

YOU WILL NOT LOSE YOUR KNOWLEDGE OF THE VEDAS IN THIS WORLD OR THE NEXT.

AT LAST THE PERIOD OF THEIR STUDIES WAS OVER.

TOMORROW WE PART AND GO OUR WAYS.

BUT I SHALL ALWAYS REMEMBER YOU.

AND I YOU.

THEY TOOK LEAVE OF GURU SANDIPANI...

...AND LEFT THE ASHRAM.

YEARS PASSED. KRISHNA BECAME THE LORD OF DWARKA AND MARRIED PRINCESS RUKMINI, THE GODDESS OF PROSPERITY INCARNATE.

SUDAMA MARRIED A BRAHMAN GIRL.

HE DID NOT CARE FOR WORLDLY PLEASURES...

...AND LIVED IN DIRE POVERTY.

EVERYONE LOVED SUDAMA AND HE HAD NO ENEMIES.

BUT HIS WIFE WAS SORELY TRIED BY THE LIFE SHE HAD TO LEAD.

SHE PATIENTLY BORE IT ALL...

THE LOVE OF MY LORD SUSTAINS ME.

...FOR SHE LOOKED UPON SUDAMA AS HER GOD.

HE IS MY GOD!

SOON CHILDREN WERE BORN TO THEM AND THE CHILDREN TOO HAD TO LEAD AN AUSTERE LIFE.

THAT NIGHT WHEN THE CHILDREN HAD SLEPT—

I BEG YOU TO BE PATIENT WITH ME, MY LORD.

DO NOT FEAR. SPEAK OUT YOUR HEART, MY GOOD LADY. DO NOT FEAR.

YOU HAVE TOLD ME THAT KRISHNA OF DWARKA IS YOUR FRIEND...

...AND HIS WIFE IS THE GODDESS OF PROSPERITY INCARNATE.

THE PROSPERITY OF DWARKA FLASHED BEFORE HER MIND'S EYE.

GO MY LORD, I BESEECH YOU, FOR THE SAKE OF OUR DEAR CHILDREN AND MEET KRISHNA.

THE VERY PROSPECT OF MEETING MY DEAR FRIEND AFTER SO MANY YEARS MAKES ME HAPPY.

I WILL GO AND SEE HIM, BUT I WILL NOT ASK FOR ANYTHING.

SUDAMA'S WIFE COULD BARELY CONCEAL HER JOY.

MY LORD! EVEN A VISIT TO KRISHNA WILL BLESS US. I AM CONTENT, MY LORD.

HOPE HAS ALREADY ENTERED MY HEART.

LORD KRISHNA, THE ALL-KNOWING, WILL UNDERSTAND. MY HUSBAND NEED NOT EVEN ASK. HE WILL GIVE.

ONE THOUGHT OCCURRED TO BOTH OF THEM AT THE SAME TIME.

I CANNOT SEND MY HUSBAND EMPTY-HANDED.

DO YOU HAVE ANYTHING IN THE HOUSE? ANYTHING WORTHY OF BEING PRESENTED TO KRISHNA?

SUDAMA'S WIFE SUDDENLY REMEMBERED SOMETHING.

MY LORD USED TO TELL ME HOW KRISHNA LOVED TO EAT POWA*.

*FLATTENED RICE.

SUDAMA TOO REMEMBERED HOW KRISHNA HAD SNATCHED SOME POWA FROM HIS HAND.

SUDAMA'S WIFE BROUGHT THE POWA TO HIM.

BUT SHE COULD FIND NOTHING TO TIE IT IN SO...

SHE TORE THE END OF HER GARMENT...

...AND HANDED THE BUNDLE OF POWA TO SUDAMA.

HERE, MY LORD.

HE TOOK LEAVE OF HIS WIFE...

...AND SET OUT ON THE JOURNEY TO DWARKA.

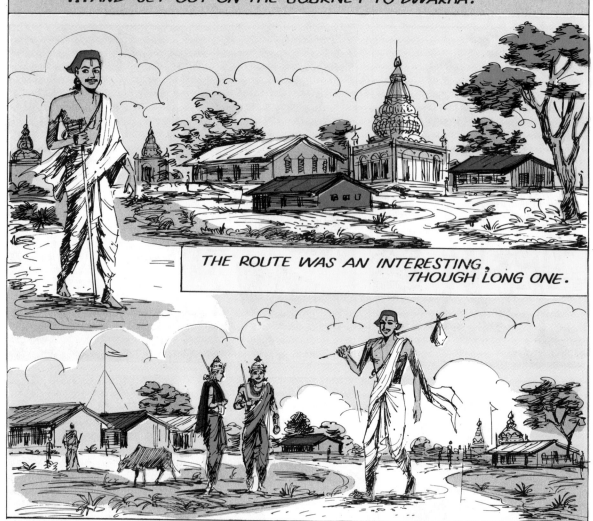

THE ROUTE WAS AN INTERESTING, THOUGH LONG ONE.

AND BEFORE HE KNEW IT, HE HAD REACHED DWARKA.

WHEN HE CAME TO THE OPEN GATES OF THE PALACE AT DWARKA, NO ONE STOPPED HIM AS HE ENTERED.

HE WALKED INTO THE PALACE GROUNDS

...AND THROUGH ROOM..

..AFTER ROOM.

AT LAST HE FOUND KRISHNA AND RUKMINI.

LOOK! WHO IS THAT?

MY DEAR FRIEND - SUDAMA!

THIS IS THE FRIEND I'VE TALKED SO MUCH ABOUT.

COME, SIT DOWN. LET ME BATHE YOUR TIRED FEET.

KRISHNA, HOW PLEASED I AM!

SO AM I.

KRISHNA APPLIED SANDALWOOD PASTE TO SOOTHE THE TIRED LIMBS OF SUDAMA.

AND PUT PIECES OF BETEL NUT INTO HIS MOUTH.

THE PALACE ATTENDANTS WONDERED.

WHAT GREAT ACT OF MERIT HAS THIS DIRTY BEGGAR IN TATTERED GARMENTS PERFORMED TO BE SO DELIGHTFULLY WELCOMED?

RUKMINI, WE MUST DO EVERYTHING POSSIBLE TO MAKE HIS STAY HERE COMFORTABLE.

AT LAST AFTER SUDAMA WAS REFRESHED —

TELL ME, HAVE YOU MARRIED?

YES, MY WIFE IS A GOOD BRAHMAN WOMAN.

YOU LEAD A HOUSEHOLDER'S LIFE, BUT YOUR HEART IS FREE FROM ATTACHMENT. DOES YOUR WIFE ACCEPT YOUR WAY OF LIFE?

SHE HAS NEVER QUESTIONED IT.

KRISHNA SAW THE RAG BUNDLE, TIED TO SUDAMA'S WAIST.

AH! YOU HAVE BROUGHT A PRESENT FOR ME.

WHEN KRISHNA SAW THAT SUDAMA WAS ASHAMED TO GIVE HIM THE BUNDLE —

THE POOREST OF GIFTS GIVEN TO ME WITH LOVE IS DEARER TO ME THAN THE RICHEST OF GIFTS GIVEN WITHOUT LOVE.

HOW CAN I GIVE MY RAG BUNDLE TO ONE WHO HAS ALL?

HE HAS NOT COME TO ASK ANYTHING FOR HIMSELF. HE HAS COME OUT OF LOVE FOR HIS WIFE AND ME!

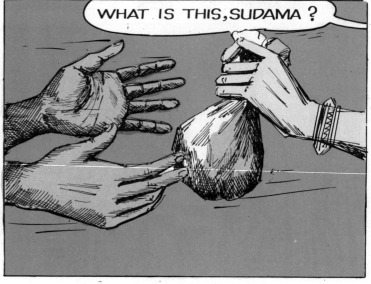

WHAT IS THIS, SUDAMA?

WHEN HE WAS ABOUT TO PICK A SECOND HANDFUL –

ENOUGH, MY LORD!

IT WAS THE DUTY OF THE GODDESS OF PROSPERITY INCARNATE TO CONTROL ITS DISTRIBUTION.

LORD! ONE MOUTHFUL IS ENOUGH TO GIVE HIM ALL HE NEEDS IN THIS WORLD AND THE NEXT.

WHAT DOES SHE MEAN? I DON'T UNDERSTAND.

SHE IS RIGHT, SUDAMA.

KRISHNA ASKED SUDAMA TO SPEND THE NIGHT IN HIS PALACE. AS SUDAMA LAY HIMSELF ON THE LUXURIOUS BED—

I AM INDEED IN HEAVEN.

THE NEXT MORNING SUDAMA TOOK LEAVE OF KRISHNA AND RUKMINI.

DON'T FORGET US, SUDAMA, WHEN YOU GO BACK HOME.

ON HIS WAY HOME, SUDAMA RELIVED HIS RECENT EXPERIENCES.

THE MEMORY OF MY MEETING WITH KRISHNA ENRAPTURES ME.

I DID NOT ASK AND HE DID NOT GIVE. BUT I AM CONTENT.

HE RECEIVED ME WITH GREAT WARMTH.

HE EMBRACED ME BECAUSE I WAS HIS FRIEND.

HE SAT ME ON THE SAME COUCH AS THE GODDESS AND IT WAS SHE WHO FANNED ME.

SUDAMA'S FEET ACHED.

I WAS RECEIVED WITH HOSPITALITY AND HE WASHED MY FEET.

HE MUST HAVE THOUGHT THAT IF HE GAVE ME WEALTH, I WOULD FORGET HIM. HE HAS SAVED ME. I AM FORTUNATE INDEED.

BUT WHEN HE NEARED HIS HOME—

WHAT IS ALL THIS?
TO WHOM DOES IT BELONG?
WHERE IS MY HUT?

SUDAMA'S WIFE AND CHILDREN CAME OUT TO RECEIVE HIM.
BUT—

MY LORD, DON'T YOU RECOGNISE ME?

FATHER, LOOK AT MY NEW CLOTHES.

AND SUDAMA UNDERSTOOD ALL.

FOR A HANDFUL OF POWA GIVEN WITH LOVE, HE HAS SHOWERED ME WITH RICHES.

WHEN SUDAMA SAW THE LUXURY WITHIN —

BUT I MUST BE CAREFUL NOT TO LET ALL THIS TURN MY HEAD!

LORD, TELL ME ALL. HOW DID THIS HAPPEN? WHAT DID YOU ASK KRISHNA?

BELIEVE ME! I ASKED FOR NOTHING. HE SHOWERED HIS LOVE AND AFFECTION ON ME. BUT...I COULDN'T ASK FOR ANYTHING. KRISHNA KNOWS ALL THAT IS IN OUR MINDS.

ANIRUDDHA

BELOVED GRANDSON OF KRISHNA

www.amarchitrakatha.com

The route to your roots

ANIRUDDHA

When Usha, daughter of the asura king, Bana, dreamt of a handsome youth, she lost her heart to him completely. Little did she know that he was Aniruddha, grandson of Krishna. Nor did she ever imagine that their love would lead to a fierce battle between the Yadava forces of Krishna and the demon army of Bana, aided by the wild hordes of Shiva.

Script
Kamala Chandrakant

Illustrations
Pratap Mulick

Editor
Anant Pai

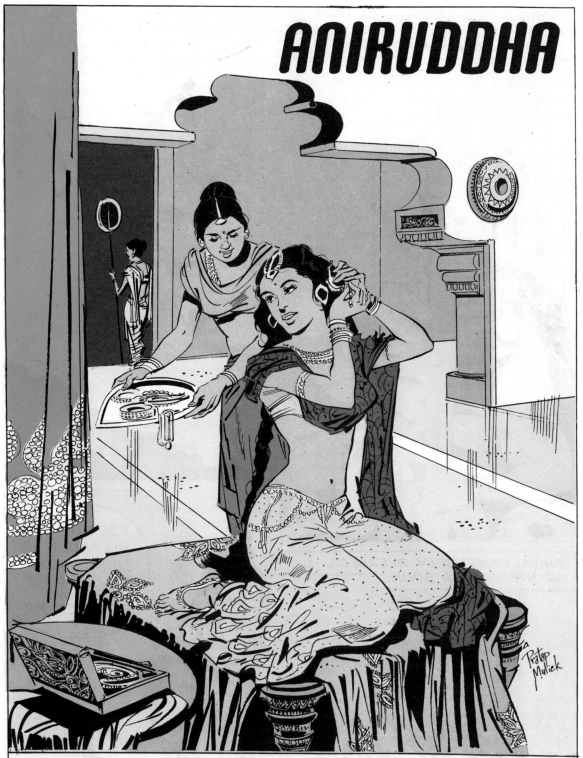

ANIRUDDHA

USHA WAS THE DAUGHTER OF THE NOBLE ASURA KING, BANA OF THE THOUSAND ARMS.

BUT AFTER SOME TIME BANA BECAME VAIN AND COMPLAINED TO SHIVA.

MY THOUSAND ARMS ARE BECOMING A USELESS BURDEN TO ME.

EVEN WITHOUT THEM THERE IS NONE EQUAL TO ME, SAVE YOU.

SHIVA, TO PUT AN END TO THIS, CURSED HIM.

O VAIN AND FOOLISH ONE, IN A FUTURE ENCOUNTER, ONE EQUAL TO ME, WILL HUMILIATE YOU.

BUT BANA WELCOMED THE CURSE AND LOOKED FORWARD TO MEETING A PEER IN FIGHT.

A FEW DAYS LATER, USHA AND HER FRIENDS WERE PICKING FLOWERS IN THEIR FAVOURITE GROVE.

IT'S GETTING WARMER AND OUR BASKETS ARE NEARLY FULL.

YES. I'M TIRED. LET'S REST.

THEY SET THEIR BASKETS DOWN AND LAY DOWN UNDER THE TREES.

AS USHA DROWSED, SHE HAD A DREAM.

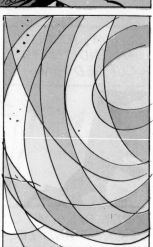

USHA WOKE UP WITH A START.

LORD! WHERE ARE YOU?

HER FRIENDS WERE AT FIRST STARTLED...

...AND THEN AMUSED. THEY BEGAN TEASING HER.

WHERE IS WHO? TELL US, USHA. DON'T BE SHY.

WHO IS THIS LUCKY LORD, WHO HAS WON YOUR HEART?

BUT CHITRALEKHA, THE DAUGHTER OF ONE OF BANA'S MINISTERS AND USHA'S CLOSE COMPANION, CAME TO HER RESCUE.

HUSH! LEAVE HER ALONE. BE OFF WITH YOU.

6

CHITRALEKHA CONSOLED HER.

DO NOT GRIEVE, MY PRINCESS. IF THIS PRINCE EXISTS, I CAN AND SHALL BRING HIM TO YOU.

BUT FIRST YOU WILL HAVE TO IDENTIFY HIM FOR ME FROM AMONG THE MANY PORTRAITS I SHALL PAINT FOR YOU.

CHITRALEKHA FIRST PAINTED A NUMBER OF GODS...

IS HE ONE OF THESE?

NO!

... GANDHARVAS ...

OR THESE?

NO!

... AND YAKSHAS.

PERHAPS THESE?

NO!

THEN WHEN AMONG THE VARIOUS PORTRAITS SHE PAINTED KRISHNA AND HIS SON PRADYUMNA —

IS HE EITHER OF THESE?

NO! BUT...

USHA WAS ABASHED, BECAUSE THEY RESEMBLED CLOSELY THE PRINCE OF HER DREAM.

AT LAST CHITRALEKHA DREW THE PORTRAIT OF ANIRUDDHA, SON OF PRADYUMNA. USHA, SUDDENLY SHY, CAST HER EYES DOWN.

THIS IS HE !

HE SHALL SOON BE HERE WITH YOU.

I SHOULD HAVE KNOWN ! SURELY, AMONG MEN, IT COULD ONLY HAVE BEEN ONE OF THE VALIANT YADAVA RACE WHO COULD HAVE DISTURBED MY PRINCESS.

THEN CHITRALEKHA WITH THE HELP OF HER YOGIC POWERS CONVEYED HERSELF...

... TO DWARAKA ...

... AND INTO THE PALACE OF ANIRUDDHA.

SHE FOUND HIM FAST ASLEEP ON HIS BED.

I AM FORTU-NATE. I SHALL DO WHAT I HAVE COME TO DO BEFORE HE WAKES UP AND RESISTS.

THUS, WHILE ANIRUDDHA SLEPT, CHITRALEKHA, USING HER YOGIC POWERS, TRANSPORTED HIM TO THE KINGDOM OF BANA...

...AND INTO THE PRESENCE OF HER DEAR PRINCESS, USHA.

HERE HE IS, MY PRINCESS. HE IS YOURS.

USHA WAS DELIGHTED.

DEAR CHITRALEKHA, YOU HAVE BROUGHT ME GREAT HAPPINESS. I SHALL EVER BE GRATEFUL TO YOU.

CHITRALEKHA WENT AWAY, LEAVING USHA WITH ANIRUDDHA.

WHERE AM I? WHO ARE YOU?

I AM USHA, THE DAUGHTER OF BANA. MY LOVE FOR YOU HAS BROUGHT YOU HERE TO THIS PALACE AS MY HONOURED GUEST.

YOU HAVE BEEN BROUGHT HERE IN SECRECY AND...

...YOU ARE FREE TO LEAVE IF YOU SO DESIRE.

BUT ANIRUDDHA WAS NOT ABLE TO TAKE HIS EYES OFF THE LOVELY USHA.

I CANNOT DREAM OF LEAVING YOU. I WOULD RATHER STAY HERE AND DELIGHT IN YOUR COMPANY.

THUS IMPRISONED BY THE TENDER ATTENTIONS OF USHA, ANIRUDDHA MARRIED HER.

SHE ENTERTAINED HIM WITH SONG AND DANCE...

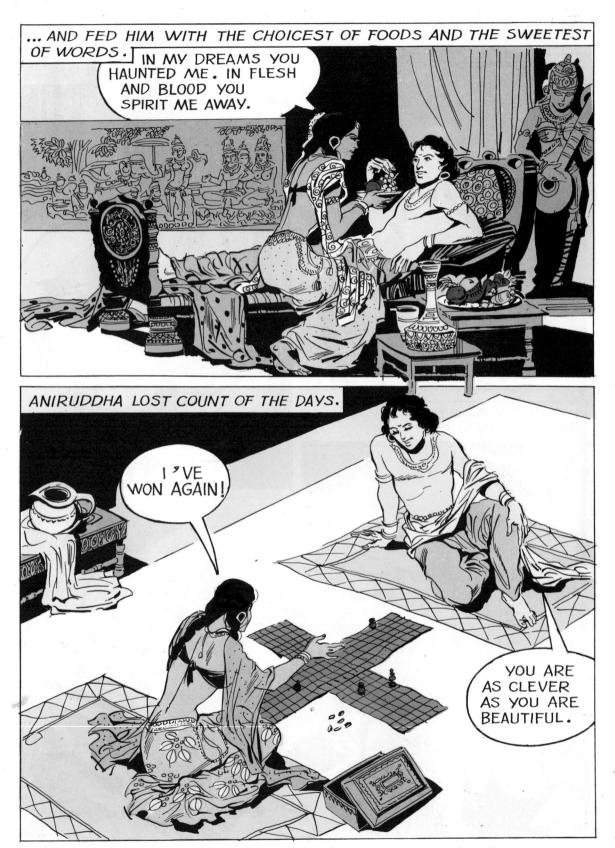

14

BUT SUCH STOLEN HAPPINESS COULD NOT LAST FOR EVER. ONE DAY—

IT IS STRANGE! THE PRINCESS HARDLY STEPS OUT OF HER ROOMS.

PERHAPS SHE IS ILL!

NO! I SUSPECT...

HUSH! LET US SEE FOR OURSELVES BEFORE WE SUSPECT ANYONE OF ANY- THING.

THE ATTENDANTS THEN SPIED ON THE PRINCESS.

THEY WENT STRAIGHT TO BANA.

O KING, FORGIVE US. WE ARE AFRAID THAT YOUR DAUGHTER'S CONDUCT...

WHAT DO YOU MEAN? **SPEAK OUT.**

SHE HAS SECRETLY MARRIED THE YADAVA PRINCE, ANIRUDDHA.

WHAT !

OH LORD, WE ARE AT A LOSS TO UNDERSTAND HOW YOUR DAUGHTER WHO IS NOT ALLOWED TO MOVE ABOUT...

BANA THUNDERED INTO USHA'S ROOM.

17

SEIZE HIM! KILL HIM!

BUT ANIRUDDHA WAS QUICK. HE GRABBED A MACE FROM ONE OF THE ATTENDANTS...

...AND SLEW ALL OF THEM BEFORE THEY COULD EVEN RE-ALISE WHAT WAS HAPPENING.

BANA WAS LIVID WITH RAGE.

USHA, LEAVE THE CHAMBER, AND DON'T LET ME SEE YOUR FACE.

BANA HELD ANIRUDDHA WITH SOME OF HIS THOUSAND ARMS AND WITH OTHERS HE BOUND HIM FROM HEAD TO FOOT, USING SERPENTS FOR ROPES.

CHITRALEKHA, WHO SAW ALL THAT HAPPENED, RAN TO USHA.

KRISHNA CALLED A COUNCIL OF ALL HIS MEN.

GET YOUR HORSES, CHARIOTS AND ARMS READY FOR BATTLE. ANIRUDDHA IS ALIVE, BUT IN DANGER. I HAVE JUST HAD NEWS OF HIM.

KRISHNA, PRADYUMNA AND SATYAKI WITH HUNDREDS OF WARRIORS SET OUT FOR BANA'S KINGDOM TO RESCUE ANIRUDDHA.

BANA'S RAGE KNEW NO BOUNDS, HE CAME OUT WITH AN EQUALLY LARGE ARMY AND A GREAT BATTLE ENSUED.

SHIVA WHO HAD PROMISED BANA HIS PROTECTION AT ALL TIMES, CAME TO HIS AID, WITH HIS SON, KARTIKEYA.

KRISHNA FOUGHT WITH SHIVA...

...PRADYUMNA WITH KARTIKEYA...

...AND SATYAKI WITH BANA.

ALL THE CELESTIALS, HEADED BY BRAHMA, THE SAGES, THE GANDHARVAS, THE APSARAS AND YAKSHAS CAME IN THEIR CHARIOTS TO WATCH THE MIGHTY BATTLE.

KRISHNA WAS EASILY THE BEST WAR-RIOR. IN NO TIME AT ALL HE DESTROYED SHIVA'S WEIRD HORDES WITH THE HELP OF JRIMBHANASTRA WHICH KEPT SHIVA STUPEFIED.

PRADYUMNA VANQUISHED KARTIKEYA WITH EASE.

BANA WAS BLIND WITH ANGER. HE LEFT SATYAKI...

...AND RUSHED AT KRISHNA.

SHIVA'S CURSE LIES HEAVY UPON ME NOW. BUT I WILL NOT GIVE UP HOPE.

WITH HIS THOUSAND ARMS, HE DREW FIVE HUNDRED BOWS AT THE SAME TIME AND SET TWO ARROWS IN EACH.

BUT KRISHNA WAS TOO QUICK FOR HIM. WITH HIS DISCUS HE CUT OFF NINE HUNDRED AND NINETY-SIX OF BANA'S ARMS, KILLED HIS CHARIOTEER AND HORSES, AND DESTROYED HIS CHARIOT.

AND THEN HE BLEW HIS CONCH IN TRIUMPH.

BANASURA TURNED TO ENTER HIS CITY GATES.

KRISHNA WAS ABOUT TO FOLLOW WHEN—

KRISHNA, BANA IS DEVOTED TO ME AND I HAVE PROMISED HIM MY PROTECTION.

I PLEAD WITH YOU TO SPARE HIM.

KRISHNA SMILED AT SHIVA.

IT IS ONLY TO HUMBLE HIM THAT I HAVE CUT OFF ALL EXCEPT FOUR OF HIS ARMS.

AND TO RELIEVE THE EARTH OF HER BURDEN, I HAVE DESTROYED HIS ARMY.

HE STILL HAS FOUR ARMS LEFT. BESIDES I GRANT HIM IMMORTALITY AND EVERLAST-ING YOUTH.

HE NEED FEAR NO ONE.

SHIVA TURNED TO ONE OF HIS SURVIVING FOLLOWERS.

BRING BANA TO US.

KRISHNA HAS PARDONED AS WELL AS BLESSED YOU. BRING HIS GRANDSON AND YOUR DAUGHTER TO HIM.

BANA LEFT THEM AND RETURNED WITH USHA AND ANIRUDDHA.

ALL DWARAKA IS ANXIOUS FOR THE RETURN OF ANIRUDDHA. WE SHALL SET OFF IMMEDIATELY.

THEN, PLACING USHA AND ANIRUDDHA IN FRONT OF HIM, THE VICTORIOUS KRISHNA, ALONG WITH PRADYUMNA AND SATYAKI, RETURNED TO DWARAKA.

KRISHNA AND SHISHUPALA

HE WAS FORGIVEN A HUNDRED TIMES

www.amarchitrakatha.com

The route to your roots

KRISHNA AND
SHISHUPALA

Shishupala's mother was shocked when she came to know that her child was destined to be killed by Krishna. She extracted a promise from him that he would forgive Shishupala a hundred offences. As he grew up Shishupala had enough reasons to be angry with Krishna. Especially after he was jilted by Princess Rukmini, in favour of the merry-eyed cowherd. He provoked Krishna repeatedly and was forgiven a hundred times. And then one day Shishupala committed his hundred and first offence.

Script	**Illustrations**	**Editor**
Kamala Chandrakant	Ram Waeerkar	Anant Pai

Cover illustration by: C.M. Vitankar

KRISHNA AND SHISHUPALA

THE HOUSE OF KING DAMA-GHOSHA OF CHEDI* WAS STEEPED IN GLOOM. WHAT SHOULD HAVE BEEN A JOYOUS EVENT TURNED OUT TO BE A NIGHTMARE. THE LONG-AWAITED SON, BORN TO DAMAGHOSHA AND HIS QUEEN, WAS A FREAK, WITH FOUR ARMS AND THREE EYES.

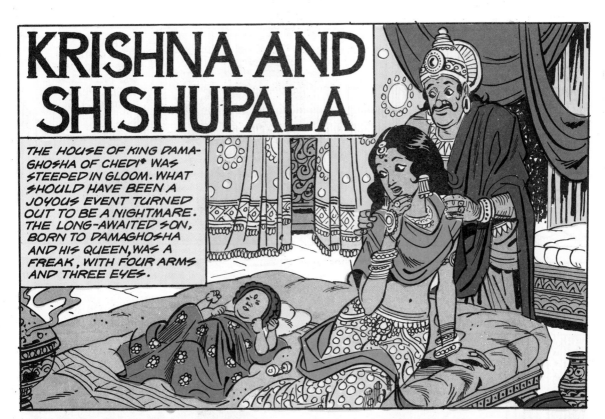

AND HE SCREAMED AND BRAYED LIKE AN ASS.

EE..AW.. EE..AW.. EE..AW

STOP HIM! WHAT HAVE WE DONE TO DESERVE THIS?

THE EVIL OMENS FRIGHTEN ME.

AH! HERE ARE THE PRIESTS AND THE ELDERS! THEY'LL TELL US WHAT TO DO.

* A VASSAL STATE OF MAGADHA

THE PRIESTS AND THE ELDERS HAD ALREADY DISCUSSED THE MATTER AMONG THEMSELVES.

ABANDON THE CHILD! THE EVIL OMENS DO NOT BODE WELL FOR THE KINGDOM...

THERE WAS A FLASH OF LIGHT AND A VOICE SUDDENLY CUT HIM SHORT.

O KING, THIS CHILD BRINGS YOU NO HARM. LOOK AFTER HIM. EVEN IF YOU ABANDON HIM, HE WILL NOT DIE...

...FOR HE IS DESTINED TO DIE ONLY AT THE HANDS OF THE ONE BORN TO SLAY HIM.

THE ANXIOUS MOTHER'S SHRIEK TORE THE SILENCE THAT FOLLOWED.

HOW WILL I KNOW THE SLAYER OF MY SON?

THE CHILD'S THIRD EYE WILL VANISH WHEN IT LOOKS UPON HIM. THE EXTRA ARMS WILL FALL OFF WHEN IT IS PLACED IN HIS LAP.

AND THE FLASH OF LIGHT WAS GONE!

MONTHS LATER, AT DWARAKA, BALARAMA CAME TO HIS BROTHER, KRISHNA, WITH NEWS.

SINCE WE KILLED KAMSA, THE EVIL SON-IN-LAW OF JARASANDHA,* NO EVENT HAS THROWN UP AS MUCH EXCITEMENT AS THIS!

AS WHAT?

AS THE BIRTH OF A MONSTER, TO OUR FATHER'S SISTER.

I SUPPOSE THEY'VE ABANDONED THE CHILD AS A FREAK?

NO! A VOICE DISSUADED THEM.

AND BALARAMA TOLD KRISHNA ALL THAT HE HAD HEARD.

* EMPEROR OF MAGADHA

3

THE CHILD HAS BEEN PLACED IN MANY A LAP. BUT SO FAR NOTHING HAS HAPPENED.

WE SHALL VISIT OUR AUNT.

I KNEW WE WOULD!

AND THE TWO BROTHERS SET OFF FOR THE CHEDI CAPITAL.

WHEN THEY REACHED THE PALACE AT CHEDI—

WELCOME, MY CHILDREN. I HAVE BEEN EXPECTING YOU TO COME TO SEE YOUR LITTLE COUSIN.

SHE WENT OUT AND RETURNED WITH THE CHILD IN HER ARMS.

HOW CAN SHE HOLD IT SO LOVINGLY? I FIND IT REPULSIVE.

ISN'T HE A LOVELY, STRONG BABY?

4

THE NEXT MOMENT —

IT'S GONE! THE THIRD EYE IS GONE!

DELIGHTED TO SEE HER SON'S FACE NORMAL, THE TREMBLING QUEEN PLACED HIM IN KRISHNA'S LAP.

THE ARMS HAVE FALLEN OFF! HOW CUTE A BABY IS HE!

IN HER EXCESSIVE JOY THE SIGNIFICANCE OF THE EVENT ESCAPED HER. BUT ONLY FOR A MOMENT.

KRISHNA, TO THINK THAT IT SHOULD BE YOU? HIS OWN COUSIN!

O KRISHNA, I AM AFRAID! TERRIBLY AFRAID.

WILL *YOU* GRANT ME A BOON? *YOU* MUST NOT REFUSE!

I'LL TRY TO BRING YOU WHAT COMFORT I CAN.

PROMISE ME THAT *YOU* WILL PARDON, FOR MY SAKE, ANY OFFENCE GIVEN BY THIS CHILD.

FOR *YOUR* SAKE, I WILL PARDON HIS OFFENCES A HUNDRED TIMES, SO DON'T GRIEVE.

HE WILL PARDON HIM A HUNDRED TIMES! MY SON IS SAFE!

6

BUT DAMAGHOSHA WAS NOT SO CERTAIN. LONG AFTER KRISHNA AND BALARAMA LEFT HE WAS DEEP IN THOUGHT.

THE MIGHT OF KRISHNA IS MATCHED BY NONE BUT JARASANDHA, WHO IS NOW KRISHNA'S SWORN ENEMY. MY SON SHALL GROW UP AT THE COURT OF MAGADHA.

SO SHISHUPALA, AS THE CHILD WAS NAMED, WAS SENT TO MAGADHA.

A FINE BOY INDEED! I SHALL MAKE YOU A LION AMONG MEN.

IN THOSE DAYS RUKMI, THE PRINCE OF VIDARBHA*, WAS AN ADMIRER OF JARA-SANDHA AND WAS OFTEN AT HIS COURT.

RUKMI, THIS BOY HERE IS SHISHUPALA, MY WARD. TRAIN HIM TO BE AS GOOD A WARRIOR AS YOU ARE!

AS THE YEARS WENT BY, RUKMI AND SHISHUPALA BECAME CLOSE FRIENDS.

IF MY FATHER GIVES RUKMINI IN MARRIAGE TO SHISHUPALA, IT WOULD PLEASE THE EMPEROR AND BRING SHISHUPALA CLOSER TO ME.

* ANOTHER VASSAL STATE OF MAGADHA

BUT THE MUCH-SOUGHT-AFTER RUKMINI HAD OTHER PLANS. ONE DAY AT DWARAKA, BALARAMA SAW A BRAHMAN LEAVE, AND KRISHNA LOOKING THOUGHTFUL.

WHO WAS THAT BRAHMAN?

HE CAME WITH A MESSAGE FROM THE PRINCESS OF VIDARBHA.

RUKMI'S SISTER, RUKMINI! THE GIRL WHO HAS WON YOUR HEART?

YES. HER BROTHER WANTS HER TO MARRY SHISHUPALA. BUT SHE HAS CHOSEN ME AND HER PARENTS SECRETLY APPROVE. SHE WANTS ME TO CARRY HER AWAY.

AND KRISHNA SET OUT FOR VIDARBHA.

MEANWHILE, SHISHUPALA HAD ALREADY RECEIVED RUKMI'S FORMAL PROPOSAL.

THIS INDEED IS AN HONOUR! TO BE OFFERED THE HAND OF PEERLESS RUKMINI! AND NO SWAYAMWARA* TO FEAR!

* A CEREMONY WHERE A MAIDEN MAKES HER CHOICE, AMONG ASSEMBLED SUITORS, BY GARLANDING HIM

BUT JARASANDHA WAS MORE CAUTIOUS.

I'LL HAVE TO BE ALERT! IT'S NO SECRET THAT KRISHNA WOULD HAVE MARRIED THE GIRL BUT FOR RUKMI. HE IS SURE TO TRY SOME WILY TRICK NOW.

IF HE DOES, IT'S GOING TO BE HARD FOR SHISHU-PALA. I SHOULD KNOW! TO AVENGE KAMSA'S DEATH, EIGHTEEN TIMES HAVE I ENCOUNTER-ED HIM AND EIGHT-EEN TIMES HAVE I FAILED!

A FEW DAYS LATER, BALARAMA RECEIVED ALARMING NEWS AT DWARAKA. HE SENT FOR HIS MEN.

THE EMPEROR HAS COMMANDED HIS ALLIES TO ASSEMBLE AT VIDARBHA. RALLY OUR ARMIES! WE'RE GOING TO VIDARBHA, TOO!

THE DAY OF THE WEDDING DAWNED. THE ASSEMBLY OF KINGS WAITED OUTSIDE THE TEMPLE WHERE RUK-MINI HAD GONE TO PRAY BEFORE THE CEREMONY.

AH! THERE SHE COMES!

SHISHUPALA IS THE LUCKIEST MAN ON EARTH!

SUDDENLY—

KRISHNA! YOU'VE COME!

SHISHUPALA WAS THE FIRST TO REACT.

IT'S THAT COWHERD, KRISHNA! HE'S CARRYING AWAY MY BRIDE! STOP HIM! STOP HIM!

BUT SO BEMUSED WERE THE KINGS THAT THEY REMAINED ROOTED TO THE SPOT, GIVING KRISHNA A GOOD LEAD.

COME ON, O KINGS! SHALVA! POUNDRAKA! DANTA-VAKTRA! PURSUE THEM! WHERE IS YOUR KSHA-TRIYA SPIRIT?

WHY DON'T YOU MOVE? ALAS! SHAME ON US WHO FLAUNT OUR BOWS! A COWHERD HAS WHISKED HER AWAY LIKE A JACKAL SNATCHING THE PREY OF A LION.

WHEN WE ARE THERE, SHISHUPALA SHALL NOT LOSE HIS BRIDE. WE'LL RESCUE THE GIRL!

RUKMI'S WORDS WENT HOME. THE KINGS CHARGED FORWARD AND SOON CAUGHT UP WITH KRISHNA. AS THEY RAISED THEIR BOWS —

WAIT! I SHALL SHOOT THE FATAL ARROW! I HAVE TO VINDICATE MY HONOUR!

BUT SHISHUPALA'S ARROW MISSED ITS MARK. HE RAISED HIS BOW AGAIN.

THIS TIME I WILL NOT MISS!

THE NEXT MOMENT—

WON'T YOU?

IT WAS BALARAMA WHO SPOKE AS HIS ARROW CUT SHISHU-PALA'S INTO TWO.

AS KRISHNA SPED AWAY WITH RUKMI IN HOT PURSUIT, BALARAMA AND HIS ARMY HELD THE OTHERS AT BAY.

A FIERCE BATTLE ENSUED. THE EMPEROR AND HIS ALLIES WERE ROUTED.

DANTAVAKTRA, ANOTHER VASSAL, SUPPORTED HIM.

AND HE'LL DO IT! COME, SHISHUPALA. DON'T GRIEVE.

TRYING TO CONSOLE THE DISTRAUGHT SUITOR AND BURNING WITH HATRED FOR HIS RIVAL ALL THE WHILE, THE VANQUISHED RETURNED TO THEIR CAPITALS.

AS HIS FATHER WAS NOW BEGINNING TO AGE, SHISHUPALA RETURNED TO CHEDI. WHEN HE ENTERED THE CAPITAL —

I HAD HOPED TO RETURN WITH A CHERISHED BRIDE BUT ALL I HAVE BROUGHT HOME IS HUMILIATION.

UNDER JARASANDHA'S PROTECTION, IN THE YEARS THAT FOLLOWED, SHISHUPALA OFTEN DELIBERATELY COMMITTED OFFENCES AGAINST THE YADAVAS — BUT ESCAPED UNPUNISHED.

HERE IS THAT RAT, SHISHUPALA! LET'S KILL HIM.

LET HIM GO, BALARAMA. REMEMBER MY PROMISE TO HIS MOTHER.

THEN ONE DAY, ONE OF SHISHU-PALA'S SPIES CAME WITH NEWS.

EMPEROR JARASANDHA HAS BEEN SLAIN!

OH, NO! WHO WAS THE WICKED MURDERER? THAT MIGHTY WARRIOR COULD NOT HAVE BEEN SLAIN IN A FAIR FIGHT.

THOUGH IT WAS PLANNED BY KRISHNA AND THE PANDAVAS, THE ACTUAL KILLING WAS BHIMA'S WORK.

THE FOUL DEED WAS DONE BY A PANDAVA! MY MOTHER'S SISTER'S CHILD! BUT WHAT DID HE HAVE AGAINST THE EMPEROR?

KING YUDHISHTHIRA WANTED TO PERFORM THE RAJASUYA SACRIFICE, FOR WHICH HE WOULD FIRST HAVE TO SECURE THE TITLE OF EMPEROR. JARASANDHA WAS THE ONLY OBSTACLE IN HIS PATH.

YUDHISHTHIRA'S FOUR BROTHERS, BHIMA ARJUNA, NAKULA AND SAHADEVA, ARE NOW ON THEIR WAY TO THE FOUR CORNERS OF THE EARTH TO SUBDUE THE KINGS. BHIMA WILL SOON BE COMING TO CHEDI.

AND IT WAS BHIMA WHO KILLED THE EMPEROR! WHAT SHOULD I DO?

AFTER PONDERING OVER THE MATTER, SHISHUPALA MADE A DECISION.

AFTER ALL, MY COUSIN YUDHISHTHIRA IS RENOWNED AS A VIRTUOUS KING. HE WILL ALWAYS BE FAIR IN HIS DEALINGS. I SHALL BECOME HIS VASSAL.

SO, WHEN BHIMA ARRIVED AT CHEDI, SHISHUPALA WENT OUT TO RECEIVE HIM.

WELCOME TO CHEDI, O MIGHTY WARRIOR! MY KINGDOM IS YOURS.

SURPRISED AND DELIGHTED BY THE WARM RECEPTION WHERE HE HAD EXPECTED HOSTILITY, BHIMA STAYED ON AT CHEDI FOR A MONTH, ENJOYING SHISHUPALA'S HOSPITALITY.

WHEN THE BROTHERS RETURNED HAVING BROUGHT ALL THE MAJOR KINGS UNDER HIS SWAY, SOME WILLINGLY, SOME BY FORCE, YUDHISHTHIRA SET A DATE FOR THE GRAND SACRIFICE IN CONSULTATION WITH KRISHNA AND THE ROYAL PRIESTS.

INVITATIONS WILL HAVE TO BE SENT OUT TO THE RISHIS, OUR COUSINS AT HASTINAPURA, THE ELDERS, AND THE VANQUISHED KINGS...

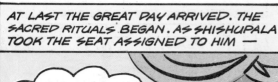

AT LAST THE GREAT DAY ARRIVED. THE SACRED RITUALS BEGAN. AS SHISHUPALA TOOK THE SEAT ASSIGNED TO HIM —

SHALVA AND DANTAVAKTRA ARE NOT HERE! DOES THE DEATH OF JARA-SANDHA STILL RANKLE IN THEM?

THE OFFICIATING PRIESTS GUIDED YUDHISHTHIRA THROUGH THE CERE-MONIES TO THE FINAL DAY WHEN THE SOMA JUICE WAS EXTRACTED.

YOU MUST NOW DECIDE WHOM YOU WILL HONOUR FIRST IN THIS ASSEMBLY OF SAGES AND KINGS.

YUDHISHTHIRA WAS AT A LOSS. HE HAD THOUGHT OF EVERYTHING BUT THIS.

THERE ARE MANY PRESENT WHO ARE WORTHY OF THE PRIME HONOUR. WHAT SHALL I DO? WHOM SHALL I CHOOSE?

WHY DOES HE HESITATE? IS THERE ANY DOUBT TO WHOM THE HONOUR SHOULD GO?

WHEN YUDHISHTHIRA DID NOT SPEAK, SAHADEVA, THE YOUNG-EST PANDAVA, STOOD UP.

I PROPOSE KRISHNA, THE PEERLESS! BY HONOURING HIM WE WILL HONOUR OURSELVES AND ALL CREATION.

AS YUDHISHTHIRA WAITED TENSELY FOR THE REACTION OF THE ASSEMBLY—

HEAR! HEAR!

WELL CHOSEN.

DEAR, DEAR KRISHNA! THOUGH NO ONE DESERVES THIS HONOUR MORE THAN YOU DO, IT IS GOOD TO SEE THAT EVERY-BODY APPROVES.

YUDHISHTHIRA ROSE...

...WASHED THE FEET OF KRISHNA...

... AND, AS WAS THE CUSTOM, SPRINKLED THE WATER IN WHICH HIS FEET HAD BEEN WASHED ON THE HEADS OF DRAUPADI AND HIS BROTHERS.

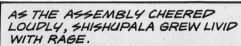

AS THE ASSEMBLY CHEERED LOUDLY, SHISHUPALA GREW LIVID WITH RAGE.

JAI! JAI!

SUDDENLY HIS VOICE CUT SHARPLY THROUGH THE CHEERS.

WAIT! HOW CAN YOU, THE ELDERS, THE WISE MEN OF THIS ASSEMBLY, SUCCUMB TO THE WHIMS OF A MERE BOY?

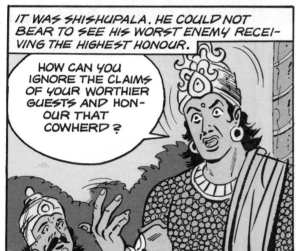

IT WAS SHISHUPALA. HE COULD NOT BEAR TO SEE HIS WORST ENEMY RECEIVING THE HIGHEST HONOUR.

HOW CAN YOU IGNORE THE CLAIMS OF YOUR WORTHIER GUESTS AND HONOUR THAT COWHERD?

FEEDING HIS FURY WITH EACH ABUSE, SHISHUPALA WENT ON.

ABANDONING THEIR OWN KINGDOM, THE YADAVAS HAVE TAKEN REFUGE IN AN ISLAND WHICH HAS NO BRAHMANS — NO VEDIC STUDIES. FROM THAT HIDEOUT THEY TYRANNISE VIRTUOUS KINGS.

HOW CAN ONE OF THIS BARBAROUS RACE BE WORTHY OF HONOUR, PARTICULARLY IN THIS AUGUST ASSEMBLY?

WHY DOESN'T KRISHNA STOP THIS MADMAN?

19

WHEN THE PANDAVAS AND THEIR ALLIES CHARGED AT SHISHUPALA TO SILENCE HIM —

SHAME ON YOU, NOBLE KSHATRIYAS, WHO WOULD DRAW YOUR SWORDS FOR A WILY COWHERD!

WAIT! SHISHUPALA IS DESTINED TO DIE AT MY HANDS. HON-OURING A PROMISE MADE TO MY AUNT, HIS MOTHER . . .

. . . I HAVE PARDONED HIM A HUNDRED TIMES. HE HAS NOW EXCEEDED THAT NUMBER. HIS TIME IS UP.

SEEING THEIR SUZERAIN FALL, THE VASSAL CHIEFTAINS OF CHEDI FLED FOR THEIR LIVES.

QUICK! LET US ESCAPE AND CARRY THE NEWS TO SHALVA.

I'LL STAY BEHIND AND BRING NEWS OF THEIR PLANS.

WHEN THE CHIEFTAINS WHO HAD FLED, REACHED SHALVA'S COURT —

SHISHUPALA HAS BEEN SLAIN!

IT WAS THAT VILE YADAVA COWHERD, KRISHNA, WHO DID IT.

SORROW AND ANGER OVERCAME SHALVA.

HE STOLE MY FRIEND'S BRIDE AND NOW HE HAS TAKEN HIS VERY LIFE. WHERE IS KRISHNA?

JUST THEN THE CHIEFTAIN WHO HAD STAYED BACK, ENTERED —

HE IS STILL AT INDRAPRASTHA. YUDHISHTHIRA ASKED HIM TO STAY ON AFTER THE SACRIFICE.

AND BALARAMA?

HE, TOO, IS AT INDRA-PRASTHA.

NOW IS THE TIME TO RAZE DWARAKA AND FULFIL MY PLEDGE. I WILL EXTERMINATE THE YADAVAS. AND LORD SHIVA WILL HELP ME DO IT.

SHALVA PERFORMED SEVERAL PENANCES TO APPEASE LORD SHIVA. WHEN SHIVA AT LAST APPEARED BEFORE HIM —

O LORD, GIVE ME A CHARIOT THAT CAN BECOME INVISIBLE AT MY COMMAND AND THAT CAN TRAVEL ON WATER, AIR AND EARTH ALIKE.

YOU SHALL HAVE IT. MAYA* WILL BRING IT TO YOU.

AS SOON AS SHALVA RECEIVED THE CHARIOT, HE ADDRESSED HIS MEN.

GET READY TO MOUNT AN ATTACK ON DWARAKA, THE CITY OF THE YADAVAS. WE WILL LEAVE FORTHWITH.

* ARCHITECT OF THE DEVAS AND ASURAS

WHEN SHALVA AND HIS ARMY REACHED DWARAKA —

YOU LAY SIEGE TO THE CITY WHILE I ATTACK FROM THE SKIES.

SHALVA DID NOT WASTE ANY TIME. SOARING INTO THE SKIES IN HIS CHARIOT, HE SHOWERED STONES, TREES, SNAKES, WATER AND EARTH OVER THE CITY, WREAKING HAVOC UPON IT.

THE CITIZENS OF DWARAKA RUSHED IN ALARM TO PRADYUMNA*.

LORD! LORD! WE ARE BEING ATTACKED... FROM THE SKIES!

* KRISHNA'S SON

23

WHERE? BY WHOM?

WE DON'T KNOW. WE CAN'T SEE ANYONE DISPATCHING WEAPONS.

THE SKIES ARE CLOAKED IN DARKNESS.

DON'T PANIC! I'LL PROTECT YOU.

AND PRADYUMNA RODE OUT.

MEANWHILE AT INDRAPRASTHA, KRISHNA AWOKE WITH A START.

BALARAMA! DWARAKA IS IN TROUBLE! WE MUST RETURN IMMEDIATELY.

UH? DWARAKA?

BIDDING YUDHISHTHIRA AND HIS BROTHERS FAREWELL, KRISHNA AND BALARAMA LEFT FOR DWARAKA.

AS THEY APPROACHED THEIR CITY —

LOOK! IT'S SHALVA! HE HAS ATTACKED THE CITY WHILE WE WERE AWAY.

GO, BALARAMA. HELP PRADYUMNA GUARD THE CITY. PROTECT FATHER. I'LL DEAL WITH SHALVA.

AS BALARAMA RODE INTO THE CITY, PRADYUMNA MET HIM.

AH! YOU'RE BACK. WE'VE ALMOST FINISHED OFF SHALVA'S ARMY. I'VE KILLED SHALVA'S MINISTER. NOW I'M GOING TO GET HIM.

NO. LEAVE HIM TO YOUR FATHER. WE'LL GUARD THE CITY AND PROTECT YOUR GRANDFATHER.

MEANWHILE, KRISHNA HAD FOUND SHALVA.

DRIVE THE CHARIOT NEAR HIS. HE IS A SKILLED MAGICIAN. SO DON'T BE FRIGHTENED BY ANYTHING YOU SEE.

IN FACT IT WAS SHALVA WHO WAS FRIGHTENED FOR A MOMENT.

IT'S KRISHNA! AND MY ARMY IS ALMOST ANNIHILATED! MY MINISTER IS DEAD. I'LL HAVE TO USE MY MOST POWERFUL WEAPON—THE SHAKTI.

AND SHALVA HURLED THE SHAKTI...

...BUT KRISHNA SMASHED IT TO BITS WITH HIS SWIFT, WELL-AIMED ARROWS.

I'LL DESTROY FOREVER THE BOW THAT SENT THOSE ARROWS AND THE HAND THAT WIELDED IT!

WITH A TRIUMPHANT ROAR, SHALVA MADE FOR KRISHNA.

STEAL MY FRIEND'S BRIDE, WOULD YOU? SLAY HIM, WOULD YOU? TODAY I SHALL SEND YOU TO THE JAWS OF DEATH — YOU WHO BOAST OF NEVER HAVING BEEN DEFEATED!

BUT THE NEXT MOMENT, KRISHNA SWUNG OUT WITH HIS MACE AND HIT SHALVA.

EE-A-A-AH!

AS SHALVA FELL KRISHNA DIPPED HIS CHARIOT IN HOT PURSUIT.

BUT THE MOMENT SHALVA'S BODY TOUCHED THE EARTH, IT VANISHED.

AND A FEW MINUTES LATER, A MAN STOOD BEFORE KRISHNA, HIS HEAD BOWED, HIS EYES STREAMING WITH TEARS.

I HAVE BEEN SENT BY DEVAKI*. O KRISHNA, SHALVA HAS CARRIED AWAY YOUR FATHER!

IT CANNOT BE TRUE! HOW COULD SHALVA DEFEAT BALA-RAMA, AND CARRY AWAY MY FATHER! BALA-RAMA, WHOM EVEN THE DEVAS AND ASURAS CAN'T DEFEAT!

SUDDENLY —

LOOK, KRISHNA! I'VE GOT YOUR FATHER! I PLAN TO KILL HIM BEFORE YOUR VERY EYES! IF YOU ARE POWERFUL ENOUGH, SAVE HIM.

SO WHAT I HEARD WAS TRUE!

* KRISHNA'S MOTHER

AND SHALVA BROUGHT HIS SWORD DOWN ON HIS CAPTIVE'S NECK.

AS SHALVA MOUNTED HIS CHARIOT AND ROSE INTO THE AIR, KRISHNA WHO WAS FOR A MOMENT STUNNED, SUDDENLY REALISED THE TRUTH.

SHALVA HAS CAST A SPELL ON ME. IT'S AN ILLUSION. THERE WAS NO MESSENGER AND MY FATHER IS SAFE.

AND LO! EVEN AS KRISHNA SAW THE TRUTH, THE CORPSE AS WELL AS THE MESSENGER VANISHED.

AH! THERE HE IS! I WILL NOT SPARE HIM NOW!

HE HAS FOUND ME OUT!

QUICK! TAKE THE CHARIOT AS CLOSE TO HIM AS YOU CAN.

IF I HAVE TO DESTROY SHALVA, I'LL FIRST HAVE TO DESTROY HIS CHARIOT.

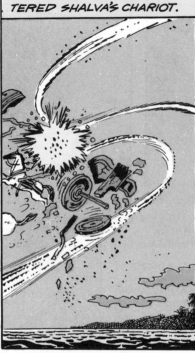

THE NEXT MOMENT, SWINGING OUT HIS MACE, WITH ONE BLOW KRISHNA SHATTERED SHALVA'S CHARIOT.

UNDAUNTED, SHALVA CAME OUT OF THE WATER . . .

. . . AND CHARGED AT KRISHNA WITH HIS MACE.

REPELLING THE ATTACK WITH ONE HAND . . .

. . . KRISHNA HELD UP THE OTHER FOR HIS DISCUS . . .

. . . AND SENT IT FLYING TOWARDS SHALVA.

SHALVA FELL, HIS HEAD SEVERED FROM THE BODY.

HAVING SLAIN ALL THE MAJOR ENEMIES OF THE YADAVAS, KRISHNA ENTERED HIS CITY CHEERED BY HIS JUBILANT SUBJECTS.

TALES OF
BALARAMA
VALIANT BROTHER OF KRISHNA

www.amarchitrakatha.com

The route to your roots

TALES OF
BALARAMA

Balarama was not only Krishna's brother, he was his right-hand man. Together they made quite a team. Balarama's amazing strength and courage made dangerous demons like Dhenukasura and Pralamba look like weaklings. He even tamed the Yamuna river which had meandered away from Vrindavan and brought it back to the people who needed it.

Script
Meera Ugra

Illustrations
Ram Waeerkar

Editor
Anant Pai

BALARAMA

RAMA AND KRISHNA SPENT THEIR CHILDHOOD IN GOKUL.

EVERY DAY, ALONG WITH THE OTHER COWHERDS OF THE VILLAGE, THE TWO BROTHERS WOULD TAKE THEIR CATTLE OUT TO THE FOREST TO GRAZE.

ONE MORNING—

RAMA! KRISHNA! LOOK! BERRIES! HUNDREDS OF THEM!

WHAT ARE WE WAITING FOR? LET'S HAVE SOME.

WAIT, RAMA!

THAT TREE GROWS IN DHENUKASURA'S TERRITORY.

NO CATTLE WHICH ENTER THAT PLACE RETURN HOME ALIVE.

FOR THAT MATTER, NOR DOES A COW-HERD.

WELL, KRISHNA?

ASSUMING THE FORM OF A WILD ASS, DHENUKA SHOT OUT OF HIS CAVE.

4

RAMA AND KRISHNA HOWEVER, STOOD WHERE THEY WERE AND WENT ON SHAKING THE TREE.

SUDDENLY —

THE NEXT MOMENT RAMA FOUND HIMSELF UP IN THE AIR.

EVEN AS HE LANDED, DHENUKA LASHED OUT AGAIN...

...BUT THIS TIME RAMA WAS READY.

WELL DONE, RAMA!

NOW LET'S EAT SOME OF THOSE BERRIES.

WHERE ARE THE BOYS?

THE BOYS SLOWLY CREPT OUT FROM BEHIND THE BUSHES.

I THOUGHT YOU HAD ALL GONE HOME!

HOW COULD WE? LEAVING...

... LEAVING THESE LUSCIOUS BERRIES BEHIND?

JUST THEN —

THUMP

THUMP

WHAT'S THAT?

THEY'RE DHENUKA'S HORDES!

DON'T PANIC. THEY HAVE COME IN SEARCH OF THEIR MASTER.

WE WILL HAVE TO HELP THEM TO FIND HIM.

AS THE CATTLE GRAZED, THE COWHERDS WRESTLED AND PLAYED GAMES TO WHILE THEIR TIME AWAY.

ONE DAY A STRANGER CAME UP TO THEM.

MAY I JOIN YOU, FRIENDS?

ONLY IF YOU CAN TEACH US A NEW GAME.

HAVE YOU EVER RUN A RACE IN PAIRS, JUMPING WITH BOTH FEET AT ONCE LIKE DEER?

NO. BUT IT SHOULD BE FUN.

WHAT DOES THE WINNER GET?

A JOY RIDE.

THE LOSER WILL HAVE TO CARRY HIM BACK TO THE STARTING-POINT.

LET'S BEGIN. NOW!

HEY! WHERE ARE YOU TAKING ME?

I AM TAKING YOU HOME...

...TO MY HOME IN THE ASURA KINGDOM. YOU WILL MAKE A GOOD SLAVE.

PRALAMBA WAS AN ASURA WHO HAD COME TO THE FOREST IN THE GUISE OF A COWHERD.

YOU ARE STRONG, HEALTHY... AND...AND...

...HEAVY. I'D BETTER ASSUME MY TRUE FORM.

YOU SHOULD BID YOUR FRIENDS GOOD-BYE. FOR YOU WILL NEVER SEE THEM AGAIN.

NEVER? OH! WELL...

KRISHNA! KRISHNA!

I AM BEING CARRIED AWAY ...BY AN ASURA...

13

THE POOR ASURA!

AS HE RAN ON, THE ASURA SUDDENLY FELT RAMA'S LEGS TIGHTENING THEIR HOLD. RAMA WAS STRANGLING HIM!

HEY! RAMA ...LET GO... AAAAH...

THE NEXT MINUTE THE ASURA FELL DEAD.

14

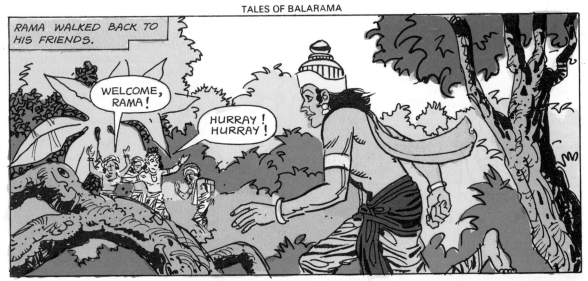

RAMA WALKED BACK TO HIS FRIENDS.

WELCOME, RAMA!

HURRAY! HURRAY!

BY EVENING, ALL GOKULA RESOUNDED WITH THE TALE OF RAMA'S STRENGTH.

NANDA, YOU ARE BLESSED INDEED!

HE WILL ACCOMPLISH GREAT FEATS.

THERE IS NONE WHO CAN MATCH YOUR MIGHT, RAMA...

...THEREFORE YOU SHALL HENCE-FORTH BE CALLED BALARAMA.

LONG LIVE BALARAMA!

THE TITLE CONFERRED BY HIS FOSTER-FATHER, NANDA, STUCK. RAMA CAME TO BE CALLED BALARAMA.

BALARAMA TAMES YAMUNA

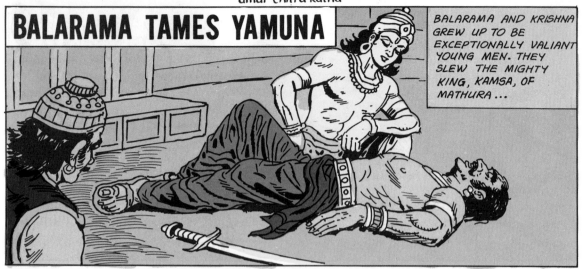

BALARAMA AND KRISHNA GREW UP TO BE EXCEPTIONALLY VALIANT YOUNG MEN. THEY SLEW THE MIGHTY KING, KAMSA, OF MATHURA...

...FREED THEIR PARENTS FROM KAMSA'S PRISON...

...AND REINSTATED THEIR MATERNAL GRANDFATHER, UGRASENA, ON THE THRONE.

WHEN BALARAMA RETURNED HOME ON A VISIT —

LOOK! IT'S BALARAMA!

BALARAMA!

WELCOME, BALARAMA!

HOW GOOD IT IS TO BE BACK HERE WITH YOU!

PROBLEMS? WHAT PROBLEM CAN THERE BE NOW?

THERE IS NO WATER.

NO WATER? WHAT ABOUT YAMUNA? SHE NEVER RUNS DRY!

YAMUNA IS MILES AWAY FROM HERE, BALARAMA.

THEN BRING HER HERE.

HOW? BY REQUESTING HER TO COME?

YOU SPEAK AS IF WE ONLY HAVE TO WISH IT AND SHE'LL COME RUSHING TO US.

...HE BROUGHT IT DOWN WITH A THUD...

...AND BEGAN DRAGGING IT BEHIND HIM.

THROUGH THE FURROW DUG BY THE PLOUGH, THE RIVER...

...RUSHED AFTER HIM...

...RIGHT UP TO THE FOREST.

THERE! YAMUNA HAS COME TO YOU!

20

BALARAMA WEDS REVATI

ONCE TWO STRANGERS ARRIVED AT DWARAKA WHERE KRISHNA AND BALARAMA NOW LIVED.

LOOK, REVATI! HOW EVERYTHING HAS CHANGED!

MEN AND WOMEN HAVE BECOME SO SMALL...

...AND SO WEAK! TEN MEN LIFTING THAT TINY LOG!

LORD BRAHMA HAD WARNED US ABOUT THIS, FATHER.

HM-M-M... YES... HE HAD. WELL, MY CHILD, LET'S FIND THE PALACE.

BUT, FATHER, IS THIS OUR CAPITAL?

LET'S ASK THOSE MEN.

BUT —

GIANTS! RUN!

WAIT! DON'T RUN AWAY!

DON'T BE AFRAID. WE WON'T HARM YOU. WE ARE FRIENDS.

F-FRIENDS?

IS THIS KUSHASTHALI?

K-KUSHASTHALI?

I BEG YOUR PARDON. IS THIS DWARAKA?

YES ...NO... I... I MEAN WE ARE VERY NEAR DWARAKA.

THEN LEAD US TO THE PALACE OF THE KING.

THERE! THAT FORTRESS IS DWARAKA.

AND A LITTLE LATER —

KING RAIVATA OF KUSHASTHALI WISHES TO SEE YOU, MAHARAJ.

LEAD HIM IN.

KING RAIVATA... KUSHASTHALI... I HAVE HEARD OF NEITHER.

HAVE YOU HEARD OF RAIVATA, SIR?

RAIVATA? AH, RAIVATA. YES... I HAVE.

THERE WAS ONE RAIVATA ...THOUSANDS AND THOUSANDS OF YEARS AGO...

THOUSANDS OF YEARS AGO?

I DON'T UNDERSTAND...

MAHARAJ, KING RAIVATA IS HERE.

UGRASENA WELCOMED THE VISITORS...

...AND HAD SPECIAL SEATS BROUGHT IN FOR THEM.

I AM RAIVATA, A GREAT-GRANDSON OF MANU. I REIGNED OVER THIS LAND CENTURIES AGO.

I BELONG TO THE FIFTH GENERATION OF MANU. MY KINGDOM WAS ANARTTA.

MY CAPITAL, KUSHASTHALI WAS SITUATED WHERE YOUR CITY NOW STANDS.

THIS IS MY DAUGHTER, REVATI. WORTHY AND VIRTUOUS, SHE IS A GEM AMONG WOMEN.

"IT WAS FOR HER SAKE THAT I LEFT MY KINGDOM AND SET OFF FOR BRAHMALOKA.

"WHEN WE REACHED THERE, WE FOUND LORD BRAHMA RAPT IN THE WORLD OF MUSIC.

WE DID NOT WANT TO DISTURB THE LORD, SO WE WAITED.

"ONLY WHEN THE MUSIC CEASED, DID I ADDRESS BRAHMA."

MY LORD, PLEASE SUGGEST A SUITABLE BRIDEGROOM FOR MY DAUGHTER.

O KING, DO YOU REALIZE HOW MUCH TIME HAS ELAPSED ON EARTH SINCE YOU LEFT IT?

TIME... OH...

...OH, YES! IT MUST BE CENTURIES! OH, HOW COULD I HAVE FORGOTTEN THAT ONE DAY IN BRAHMALOKA IS EQUAL TO MANY CENTURIES ON EARTH!

WHAT WILL HAPPEN NOW, LORD BRAHMA? WHO WILL MARRY MY DAUGHTER? PLEASE HELP ME.

DO NOT BE DISTURBED, KING RAIVATA.

THEN BRAHMA ASKED ME TO GO BACK TO MY OWN KINGDOM WHERE I WOULD FIND A WIELDER OF THE PLOUGH...

...WHO WOULD MARRY MY DAUGHTER.

I CERTAINLY WOULD.

BALARAMA

BUT SHE IS A BIT TOO TALL FOR ME. I'LL HAVE TO DO SOMETHING ABOUT IT. I'LL...

BALARAMA

EH!

WELL, BALARAMA?

MAHARAJ...

YES, BALARAMA?

PLEASE REQUEST THE PRINCESS TO TOUCH MY PLOUGH SHARE WITH HER TOE.

THE PRINCESS DID SO.

AND LO! SHE GREW SHORTER AND SHORTER TILL —

PERFECT! THE MATCH IS JUST PERFECT!

LATER, ON AN AUSPICIOUS DATE, BALARAMA AND REVATI WERE UNITED IN MARRIAGE AMIDST GREAT REJOICING.

Suppandi and his friends are all packed!

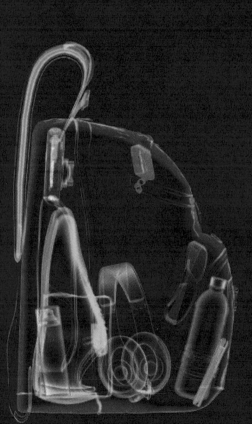
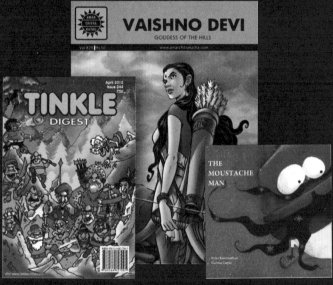 

Available on the iPad!

ANANT PAI
MASTER STORYTELLER
Vol.834 | Rs 50

A chemical engineer by profession, Anant Pai gave up his job to follow his dream, a dream that led to the birth of Amar Chitra Katha and Tinkle.

Anant Pai - Master Storyteller traces the story of the man who left behind a legacy of learning and laughter for children. ACK Media's new iPad app brings alive a new reading experience using panel-by-panel view technology, created in-house.